REALLY EASY GUITAR

DISNEY HITS

22 SONGS WITH CHORDS, LYRICS & GUITAR GRIDS

ISBN 978-1-70515-964-4

Visit Hal Leonard Online at
www.halleonard.com

World headquarters, contact:
Hal Leonard
7777 West Bluemound Road
Milwaukee, WI 53213
Email: info@halleonard.com

In Europe, contact:
Hal Leonard Europe Limited
1 Red Place
London, W1K 6PL
Email: info@halleonardeurope.com

In Australia, contact:
Hal Leonard Australia Pty. Ltd.
4 Lentara Court
Cheltenham, Victoria, 3192 Australia
Email: info@halleonard.com.au

GUITAR NOTATION LEGEND

Chord Diagrams

CHORD DIAGRAMS graphically represent the guitar fretboard to show correct chord fingerings.

- The letter above the diagram tells the name of the chord.
- The top, bold horizontal line represents the nut of the guitar. Each thin horizontal line represents a fret. Each vertical line represents a string; the low E string is on the far left and the high E string is on the far right.
- A dot shows where to put your fret-hand finger and the number at the bottom of the diagram tells which finger to use.
- The "O" above the string means play it open, while an "X" means don't play the string.

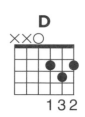

Tablature

TABLATURE graphically represents the guitar fingerboard. Each horizontal line represents a string, and each number represents a fret.

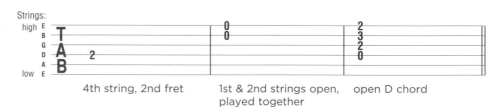

4th string, 2nd fret   1st & 2nd strings open, played together   open D chord

Definitions for Special Guitar Notation

HAMMER-ON: Strike the first (lower) note with one finger, then sound the higher note (on the same string) with another finger by fretting it without picking.

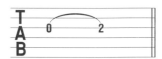

PULL-OFF: Place both fingers on the notes to be sounded. Strike the first note and without picking, pull the finger off to sound the second (lower) note.

LEGATO SLIDE: Strike the first note and then slide the same fret-hand finger up or down to the second note. The second note is not struck.

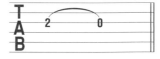

SHIFT SLIDE: Same as legato slide, except the second note is struck.

Additional Musical Definitions

N.C.

- No chord. Instrument is silent.

- Repeat measures between signs.

Beauty and the Beast

from BEAUTY AND THE BEAST
Music by Alan Menkin
Words by Howard Ashman

(Capo 1st Fret)

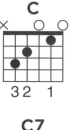 C
 G7sus4
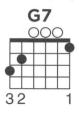 G7
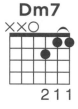 Em
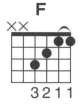 F
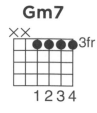 Gm7

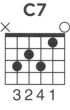 C7
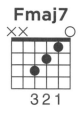 Fmaj7
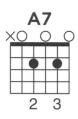 Dm7
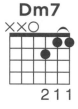 Am7
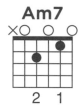 B♭
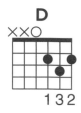 D

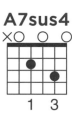 A7sus4
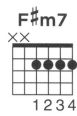 A7
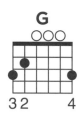 F#m7
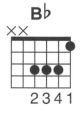 G
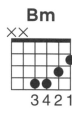 D7
 Bm

INTRO

Slow

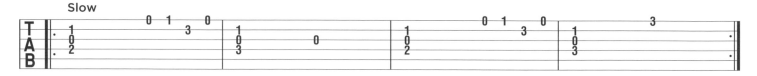

VERSE 1

C   G7sus4 G7
Tale as old as time,

C   G7sus4 G7
true as it can be.

C   Em
Barely even friends,

            F   G7sus4
then somebody bends unexpectedly.

C   G7sus4
Just a little change.

C   Gm7
Small, to say the least.

C7   Fmaj7
Both a little scared,

       Em   Dm7
neither one prepared.

G7   C   G7sus4
Beauty and the Beast.

BRIDGE

                   Em   F
Ever just the same,

                 Em   F

ever a surprise.

               Em
Ever as before,

         Am7   **B♭   C**

ever just as sure as the sun will rise.

VERSE 2

D   **A7sus4 A7**
  Tale as old as time,

D   **A7sus4 A7**
  tune as old as song.

D   **F♯m7**
  Bittersweet and strange,

                G

finding you can change,

            A7sus4 A7
learning you were wrong.

D   **A7sus4 A7**
  Certain as the sun

D   **Am7**
  rising in the East,

D7   **G**
tale as old as time,

            Em
song as old as rhyme.

A7   **D**
Beauty and the Beast.

Bm   **G**
  Tale as old as time,

          Em
song as old as rhyme.

A7
Beauty and the

OUTRO

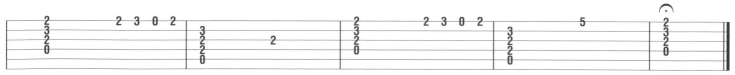

Beast.

Can You Feel the Love Tonight

from THE LION KING
Music by Elton John
Words by Tim Rice

(Capo 3rd Fret)

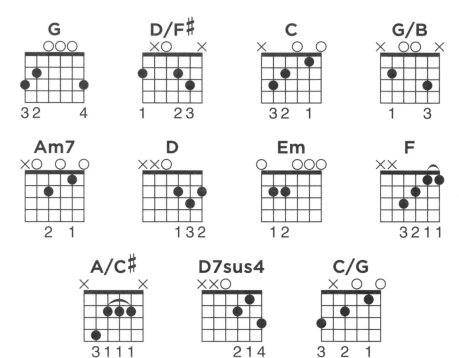

INTRO

Slow

| G   D/F# | C   G | C   G/B | D/F# G   Am7 G/B ||

VERSE 1

C   G/B C   G/B
There's a calm surrender to the rush of day,

C   G/B   Am7   D
when the heat of a rolling wind can be turned away.

C   G/B   C   G/B
An enchanted moment, and it sees me through.

C   Em   F   D
It's enough for this restless warrior just to be with you.

CHORUS

```
        G          D/F#  Em      C
And can you feel the love tonight?

G          C     A/C#  D
  It is where we      are.

C          G/B       Em         C
  It's enough for this wide-eyed wanderer.

Am7 G/B C   A/C#   D
That  we  got this far.

        G          D/F#  Em      C
And can you feel the love tonight?

G            C  A/C#  D
  How it's laid to    rest?

C          G/B       Em         C
  It's enough to make kings and vagabonds

   Am7  G/B  C    D7sus4  C/G  G
Believe  the  ver - y best.
```

REPEAT INTRO

VERSE 2

```
C               G/B      C             G/B
There's a time for everyone if they only learn

C               G/B     Am7              D
that the twisting kaleidoscope moves us all in turn.

C                  G/B  C             G/B
There's a rhyme and reason to the wild outdoors

C                  Em             F             D
when the heart of this star-crossed voyager beats in time with yours.
```

REPEAT CHORUS

OUTRO

```
C          G/B       Em         C
  It's enough to make kings and vagabonds

   Am7  G/B  C    D7sus4  C/G  G
Believe  the  ver - y best.
```

Colors of the Wind

from POCAHONTAS
Music by Alan Menken
Words by Stephen Schwartz

(Capo 1st Fret)

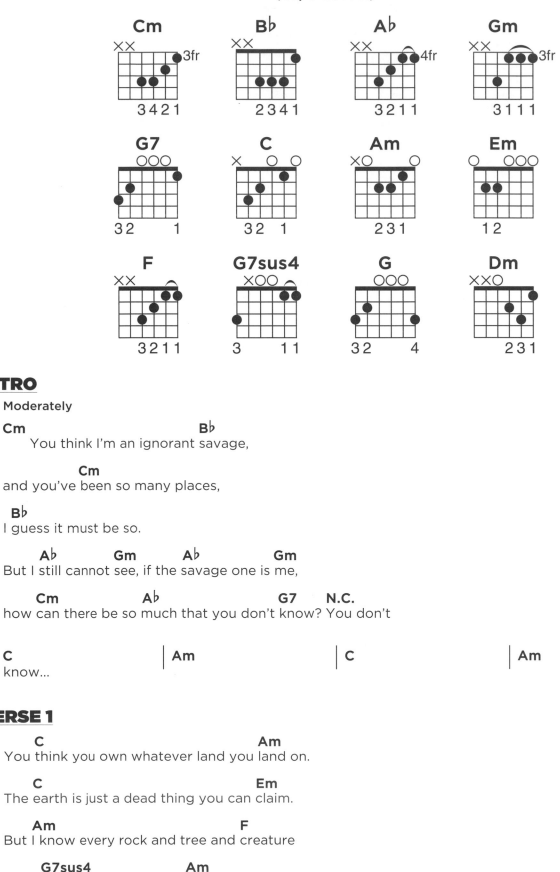

INTRO

Moderately

Cm   Bb
     You think I'm an ignorant savage,

             Cm
and you've been so many places,

  Bb
I guess it must be so.

      Ab   Gm   Ab   Gm
But I still cannot see, if the savage one is me,

    Cm   Ab   G7   N.C.
how can there be so much that you don't know? You don't

| C | Am | C | Am |
know...

VERSE 1

    C   Am
You think you own whatever land you land on.

    C   Em
The earth is just a dead thing you can claim.

  Am   F
But I know every rock and tree and creature

    G7sus4   Am
has a life, has a spirit, has a name.

VERSE 2

```
          C                         Am
You think the only people who are people

          C                         Em
are the people who look and think like you,

    Am                         F
But if you walk the footsteps of a stranger

        G7sus4                      C
you'll learn things you never knew you never knew.
```

CHORUS 1

```
          Am                    Em       F
Have you ever heard the wolf cry to the blue corn moon,

    Am                      Em
or asked the grinning bobcat why he grinned?

        F           G          C        Am
Can you sing with all the voices of the mountain?

        F                           G7sus4
Can you paint with all the colors of the wind?

        F             G7sus4
Can you paint with all the colors of the
```

```
| C                | Am              | C              | Am
wind?
```

VERSE 3

```
          C                         Am
Come run the hidden pine trails of the forrest,

          C                         Em
come taste the sun-sweet berries of the earth.

      Am                  F
Come roll in all the riches all around you,

        G7sus4                      Am
and for once never wonder what they're worth.
```

VERSE 4

```
          C                         Am
The rainstorm and the river are my brothers.

        C                         Em
The heron and the otters are my friends.

      Am                      F
And we are all connected to each other

      Dm      G7sus4         C
in a circle, in a hoop that never ends.
```

BRIDGE

```
Em  F              C           Am
How high does the sycamore grow?

         Bb                      F      G      F
If you cut it down, then you'll never know.
```

CHORUS 2

```
G         Am                      Em          F
And you'll never hear the wolf cry to the blue corn moon,

    Am                        Em
for whether we are white or copper-skinned,

        F           G           C          Am
we need to sing with all the voices of the mountain,

       F                    G
need to paint with all the colors of the wind.

        Dm          G          Em
You can own the earth and still all you'll own is earth

    F         Am          F
until you can paint with all the colors of the
```

```
| C            | Am          | F          | G          | C          |            ||
wind.
```

Do You Want to Build a Snowman?

from FROZEN
Music and Lyrics by Kristen Anderson-Lopez and Robert Lopez

(Capo 1st Fret)

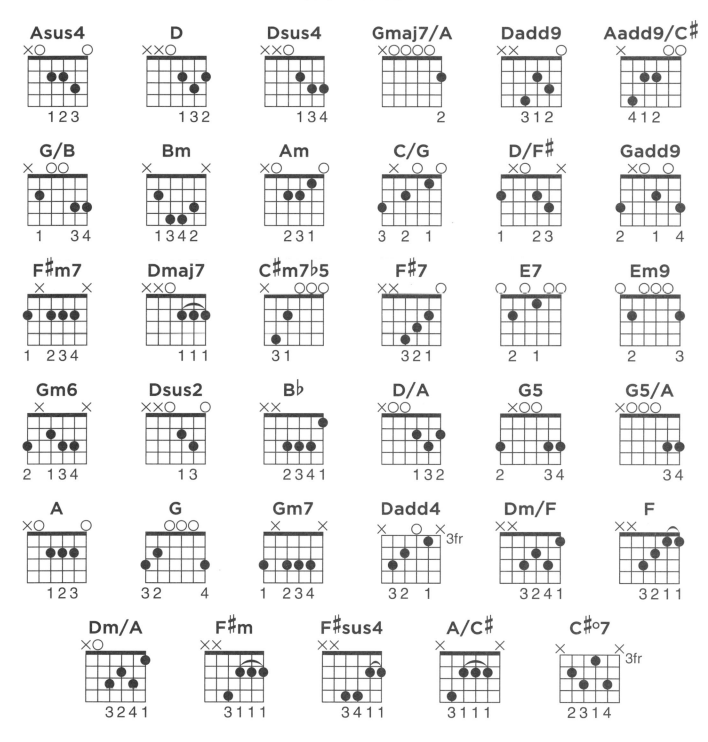

INTRO

Moderately fast

| Asus4 D Dsus4 | Asus4 D Dsus4 | Asus4 D Dsus4 | Asus4 D Dsus4 | Gmaj7/A |

(Little Anna:) Elsa?   (Knocking)

VERSE 1

             Dadd9
Do you want to build a snowman?

             Aadd9/C♯
Come on, let's go and play!

         G/B   **Bm**
I never see you anymore. Come out the door!

           Am **C/G** **D/F♯**
It's like you've gone away.

            Gadd9
We used to be best buddies,

     F♯m7   **Dmaj7**
and now we're not.

  C♯m7♭5   **F♯7**   **Bm**
I wish you would tell me why.

E7 **N.C.**   **Em9**
   Do you want to build a snowman?

          Gm6
It doesn't have to be a snowman. (Little Elsa:) Spoken: Go away, Anna. (Little Anna:) Sung: Okay.

INTERLUDE 1

| D | Dsus4 | Dsus2 | D | Dsus4 | Dsus2 | D | Dsus4 | Dsus2 | D | Dsus4 | Dsus2 |

| B♭ | D/A | | B♭ | D/A | | D | Dsus4 | Dsus2 | D | Dsus4 | Dsus2 |

| G5 | | | G5/A | | B♭ | D/A | | A |

VERSE 2

           N.C.   **D**
(Young Anna:) Do you want to build a snowman?

           Aadd9/C♯
Or ride our bikes around the halls?

           G/B
I think some company is overdue.

         Bm   **Am**   **N.C.**
I've started talking to the pictures on the walls. *Spoken: Hang in there, Joan!*

        G   **D/F♯**
Sung: It gets a little lonely, all these empty rooms,

  F♯7   **Bm**   **E** **N.C.**
just watching the hours tick by.   (Click tongue)

INTERLUDE 2

Bb			Gm7		
Bb					
N.C.			D Dsus4 Dsus2	D Dsus4 Dsus2	
D Dsus4 Dsus2	D Dsus4 Dsus2	Dadd4			
Gm7	Gm6	Dm/F	A		
Gm7	Gm6	Dm/F	F		
Gm7		Dm/A			
Bb					
A					

N.C.	

(Knocking) (Anna:) Spoken: Elsa?

VERSE 3

                              Dsus2
Sung: Please, I know you're in there.

                              Aadd9/C#
People are asking where you've been.

                             G/B
They say, "Have courage," and I'm trying to.

          Bm   **F#m F#sus4**
I'm right out here for you, just let me in.

F#m   **G**   **A/C#**   **D**
    We only have each other, it's just you and me.

C#m7b5   **C#o7** **Bm**
What are we gonna do?

E7   **N.C.**   **D/F#**
    Do you want to build a snowman?

G	N.C. G	A	N.C.		

OUTRO

N.C. Bm	G	N.C. Bm	G	N.C. (D)	

Cruella De Vil

from 101 DALMATIANS
Words and Music by Mel Leven

(Capo 1st Fret)

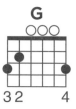
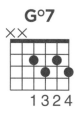
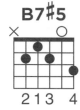
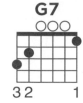
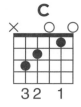
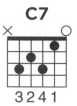

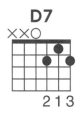
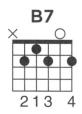

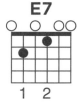

VERSE 1

Slow

   G   G7   C   C7
Cruella De Vil, Cruella De Vil,

   G   G7   C   C7
if she doesn't scare you, no evil thing will.

   G   G°7   B7♯5 E7
To see her is to take a sudden chill.

   E♭7   D7
Cruella, Cruella.

   G   G°7   B7♯5 E7
She's like a spider waitin' for the kill.

   E♭7   D7   G
Look out for Cruella De Vil.

BRIDGE

   B7   Em
At first you think Cruella is a devil,

   B7   Em
but after time has worn away the shock,

   A
you come to realize you've seen her kind of eyes

E♭9   D7
watching you from underneath a rock.

VERSE 2

    G   G7   C   C7

This vampire bat, this inhuman beast,

    G   G7   C   C7

she ought to be locked up and never released.

    G   G°7   B7♯5 E7

The world was such a wholesome place until

    E♭7   D7   G

Cruella, Cruella De Vil.

A Dream Is a Wish Your Heart Makes

from CINDERELLA
Music by Mack David and Al Hoffman
Words by Jerry Livingston

(Capo 3rd Fret)

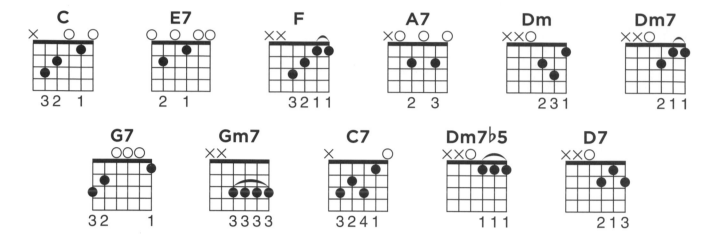

VERSE 1

Slow

    C   E7   F   A7
A dream is a wish your heart makes when you're fast asleep.

    Dm   Dm7
In dreams you will lose your heartaches,

     G7   C   Dm7   G7
whatever you wish for, you keep.

     C
Have faith in your dreams and someday

     Gm7   C7   F
your rainbow will come smiling through.

  N.C.   Dm7   Dm7b5
No matter how your heart is grieving,

    C   D7
if you keep on believing,

    Dm7   G7   C
the dream that you wish will come true.

Into the Unknown

from FROZEN 2
Music and Lyrics by Kristen Anderson-Lopez and Robert Lopez

(Capo 1st Fret)

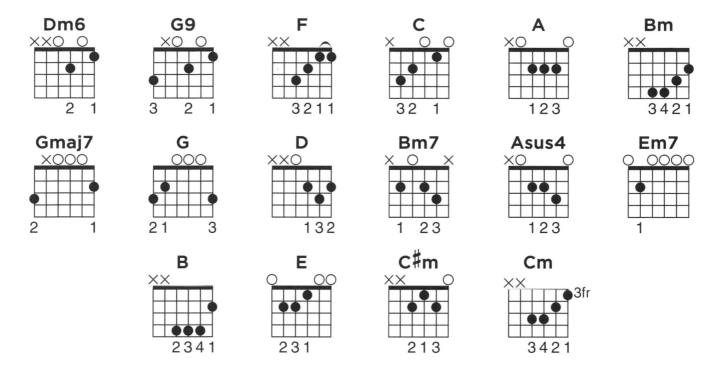

INTRO

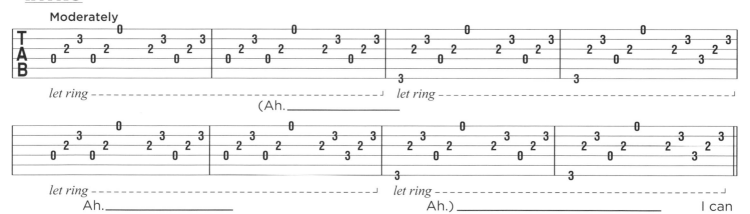

(Ah. _____

Ah. _____

Ah.) _____ I can

VERSE 1

Dm6
hear you, but I won't.

        G9
Some look for trouble while others don't.

    F   **C**
There's a thousand reasons I should go about my day

    F   **C**
and ignore your whispers, which I wish would go away... Oh.

Dm6   **G9**
   (Ah.) Oh.   (Ah.)

VERSE 2

       Dm6
You're not a voice, you're just a ringing in my ear,

    G9
and if I heard you, *which I don't*, I'm spoken for, I fear.

F   **C**
Ev'ryone I've ever loved is here within these walls.

    G9   **A**
I'm sorry, secret siren, but I'm blocking out your calls.

PRE-CHORUS 1

    Bm
I've had my adventure. I don't need something new!

    Gmaj7   **G**
I'm afraid of what I'm risking if I follow you into the un -

CHORUS 1

D   **G**   **Bm7**
known...   into the unknown...   into the unknown!

G
  (Ah. ____   Ah.) ____

VERSE 3

       Dm6
What do you want? 'Cause you've been keeping me awake.

    G9   **N.C.**
Are you here to distract me so I make a big mistake?

        F   **C**
Or are you someone out there who's a little bit like me?

    G   **Asus4**   **N.C.**
Who knows deep down I'm not where I'm meant to be?

PRE-CHORUS 2

    Bm
Ev'ry day's a little harder as I feel my power grow!

Gmaj7   **G**   **Em7**   **N.C.** **Gmaj7**
Don't you know there's part of me that longs to go...   into the un -

CHORUS 2

D   **G**   **Bm7**
known?   Into the unknown...   into the unknown!

G
  (Ah. ____   Ah.) ____

BRIDGE

               A   G

Oh, are you out there? Do you know me? Can you feel me? Can you show me?   Ah, ____

INTERLUDE

| B | | E | |
```
_____ ah, _____ ah, _____
```
| B | | E | |
```
____ ah, _____ ah, _____ ah. _____
```

OUTRO

C#m   A
Where are you going? Don't leave me alone!

C   Cm   N.C.   B   N.C.
How do I follow you   into the unknown?

Go the Distance

from HERCULES
Music by Alan Menken
Lyrics by David Zippel

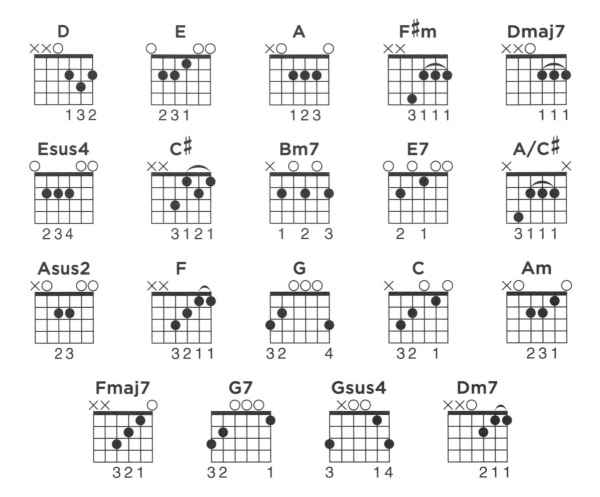

VERSE 1

Slow

```
        D E A         D E A
I have of - ten dreamed of a far off place
```

```
        D   E   F#m            Dmaj7    Esus4  E
where a great warm welcome will be waiting for me.
```

```
        D   E   A            D   E   F#m
Where the crowds will cheer when they see my face,
```

```
        D   C#  F#m      Dmaj7           Esus4  E
and a voice keeps saying this is where I'm meant to be.
```

CHORUS

```
        A        Bm7
I will find my way.

A                E
I can go the distance.

        A        Bm7
I'll be there someday

A       E       E7
if I can be strong.

        A/C#   D       F#m       Bm7
I know every mile will be worth my while.

        D   E   A
I would go most anywhere

    Dmaj7 Esus4 E   A   Asus2   D
to feel like I       belong.
```

INTERLUDE

```
| A     Asus2     D          | A     Asus2     D          |          |          |

| F     G     C              | F     G     C              | F     E     Am       |

| Fmaj7           | G        | F     G     C     G7       |
```

OUTRO

```
        C        F
I am on my way.

Gsus4         G
I can go the distance.

        C        F
I don't care how far,

Gsus4         G
somehow I'll be strong.

        C        F       Am      Dm7
I know every mile will be worth my while.

        F   G   C
I would go most anywhere

    Fmaj7   Gsus4   C
to find where I       belong.
```

God Help the Outcasts

from THE HUNCHBACK OF NOTRE DAME
Music by Alan Menken
Lyrics by Stephen Schwartz

(Capo 4th Fret)

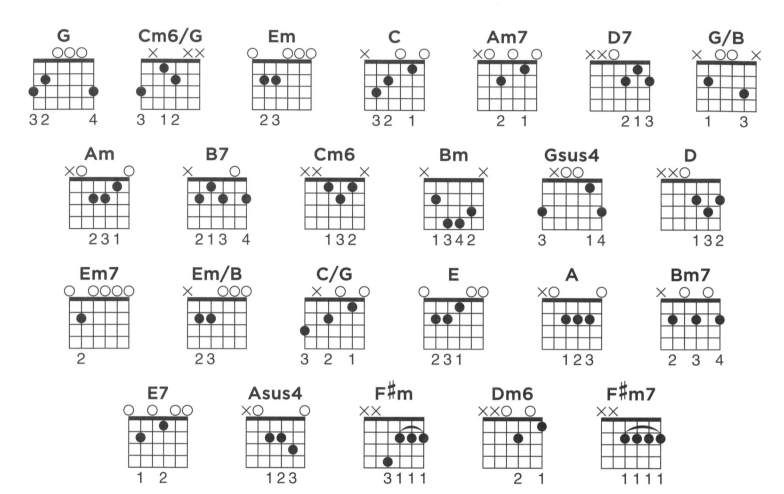

VERSE 1

Slow

          N.C.   G   Cm6/G   G
Esmerelda: I don't know if You can hear me or if You're even there.

Em   **C**   **Am7**   **D7 G/B**
I don't know if You would listen to a gypsy's prayer.

Em   **Am**   **D7**   **B7 Em**
Yes, I know I'm just an outcast, I shouldn't speak to   You.

Cm6   **G**   **Bm** **D7**
Still, I see Your face and won - der   were You once an outcast

INTERLUDE 1

| G | Cm6/G | G | Cm6/G |
too?

CHORUS

```
G                        C
God help the outcasts, hungry from birth.

Am7           D7         Gsus4  G
Show them the mercy they don't   find on earth.

Em                       Am
God help my people, they look to You still.

Cm6        G           Am      D7  G  Cm6/G
God help the outcasts or nobod - y     will.
```

VERSE 2

```
                    G      Cm6/G        Em
Parishioners: I ask for wealth,      I ask for fame.

          C       D         G      B7
I ask for glory to shine on my name.

          Em  Em7        C    Em/B
I ask for love       I can possess.

          Am7        C/G     D    E
I ask for God and His angels to bless me.
```

OUTRO

```
A              D
I ask for nothing. I can get by,

   Bm7       E7        Asus4   A
but I know so many less luck  -   y than I.

F♯m               A     Bm
Please help my people, the poor and the downtrod.

Dm6        A        E7       F♯m
I thought we all were the children of God.

Bm7        A        E7
God help the outcasts, children of
```

```
| A              | Dm6            | A          | F♯m         |      |
  God.
| F♯m7           | D              | E          | A           |      ||
```

Hakuna Matata

from THE LION KING
Music by Elton John
Lyrics by Tim Rice

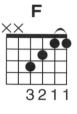
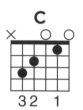
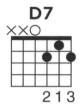
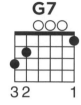
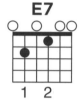

F · C · D7 · G7 · E7 · Am

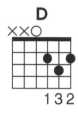
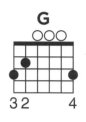
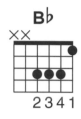
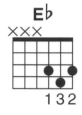
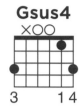

D · G · B♭ · E♭ · Gsus4

CHORUS 1

Moderately

     N.C.   F   C
Timon: Hakuna matata... what a wonderful phrase!

               F   D7   G7
Pumbaa: Hakuna matata... ain't no passing craze.

     E7   Am   F   D
Timon: It means no worries for the rest of your days.

                    C   G
Timon & Pumbaa: It's our problem-free philosophy.

     N.C.   C
Timon: Hakuna matata.

VERSE 1

               B♭   F   C
Timon: Why, when he was a young warthog...

          B♭ F   C
Pumbaa: When I was a young warthog!

     N.C.
Timon: Very nice. Pumbaa: Thanks.

       E♭   F
Timon: He found his aroma lacked a certain appeal.

     C   G
He could clear the savannah after ev'ry meal!

       B♭   F   C
Pumbaa: I'm a sensitive soul,   though I seem thick-skinned.

     E♭   F   G
And it hurt that my friends never stood down wind!

BRIDGE

                    C
Pumbaa: And oh, the shame! (Timon: He was ashamed.)

                          G
Pumbaa: Thought of changin' my name. (Timon: Oh, what's in a name?)

                    Bb
Pumbaa: And I got downhearted, (Timon: How did ya feel?)

                    N.C.
Pumbaa: every time that I... Timon: Hey, Pumbaa! Not in front of the kids! Pumbaa: Oh, sorry.

CHORUS 2

                 N.C.   F   C
Timon & Pumbaa: Hakuna matata... what a wonderful phrase!

                 F   D7   G7
Pumbaa: Hakuna matata... ain't no passing craze.

      E7   Am   F   D
Simba: It means no worries for the rest of your days.

                   C   G
Timon & Simba: It's our problem-free philosophy.

N.C.   C   F   G
    Hakuna matata.

INTERLUDE

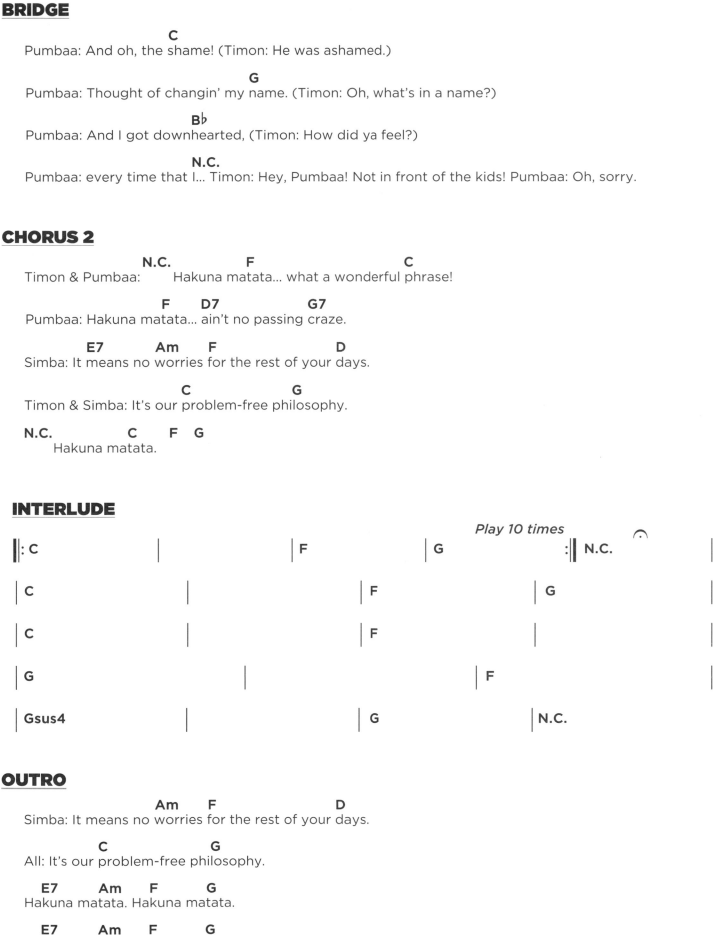

OUTRO

                Am   F   D
Simba: It means no worries for the rest of your days.

         C   G
All: It's our problem-free philosophy.

  E7   Am   F   G
Hakuna matata. Hakuna matata.

  E7   Am   F   G
Hakuna matata. Hakuna matata. Hakuna ma -

How Far I'll Go

from MOANA
Music and Lyrics by Lin-Manuel Miranda

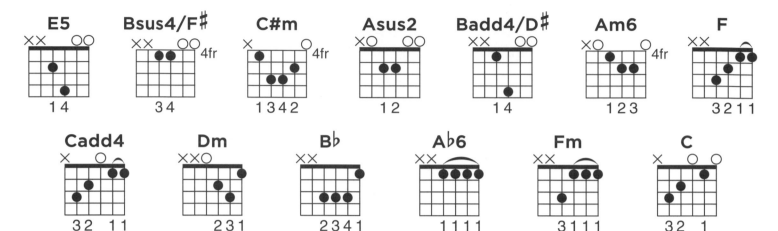

VERSE 1

Moderately

E5   Bsus4/F#   C#m
I've been staring at the edge of the water long as I can remember,

        Asus2
never really knowing why.

E5   Bsus4/F#   C#m
I wish I could be the perfect daughter, but I come back to water,

        Asus2
no matter how hard I try.

     C#m
Ev'ry turn I take, ev'ry trail I track,

    Badd4/D#
Ev'ry path I make, ev'ry road leads back

     E5
to the place I know where I cannot go,

    Am6
where I long to be.

CHORUS 1

     E5   Bsus4/F#
See the line where the sky meets the sea? It calls me.

      C#m   Asus2
And no one knows how far it goes.

     E5   Bsus4/F#
If the wind in my sail on the sea stays behind me,

      C#m   Am6
one day I'll know. If I go, there's no telling how far I'll

VERSE 2

E5   Bsus4/F#   C#m
go. I know ev'rybody on this island seems so happy on this island.

                   Asus2
Ev'rything is by design.

E5   Bsus4/F#   C#m
I know ev'rybody on this island has a role on this island,

                   Asus2
so maybe I can roll with mine.

       C#m
I can lead with pride, I can make us strong,

         Badd4/D#
I'll be satisfied if I play along.

         E5
But the voice inside sings a diff'rent song.

         Am6
What is wrong with me?

CHORUS 2

         E5   Bsus4/F#
See the light as it shines on the sea? It's blinding.

           C#m   Asus2
But no one knows how deep it goes.

         E5   Bsus4/F#
And it seems like it's calling out to me, so come find me

         C#m   Am6
and let me know. What's beyond that line? Will I cross that line?

CHORUS 3

         F   Cadd4
See the line where the sky meets the sea? It calls me.

         Dm   Bb
And no one knows how far it goes.

       F   Cadd4
If the wind in my sail on the sea stays behind me,

         Dm   Ab6 Fm Bb C
one day I'll know how far I'll go.

I See the Light

from TANGLED
Music by Alan Menken
Lyrics by Glenn Slater

(Capo 3rd Fret)

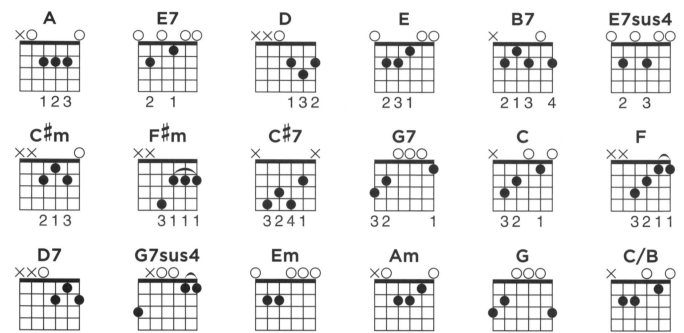

INTRO

Moderately

let ring throughout

VERSE 1

```
A              E7           A
All those days, watching from the windows,

                E7           A
all those years, outside looking in.

D         A         D     E
All that time, never even know - ing

A        B7        E7sus4  E7
just how blind I've been.

A         E7            A
Now I'm here, blinking in the starlight.

          E7           A
Now I'm here, suddenly I see.

D              C#m
Standing here, it's, oh, so clear

   F#m       B7        E7sus4  E7
I'm where I'm meant to be.
```

CHORUS 1

      D   A   E7   A
And at last I see the light, and it's like the fog has lifted.

      D   A   C♯7   F♯m
And at last I see the light, and it's like the sky is new.

        D   A   C♯m   D
And it's warm and real and bright, and the world has somehow shifted.

A   E7   A   D   E7 A   E7sus4 E7 G7
All at once ev'rything looks different, now that I see you.

VERSE 2

C   G7   C
All those days, chasing down a daydream.

         G7   C
All those years, living in a blur.

F   C   F   G7
All that time, never truly see - ing

C   D7   G7sus4 G7
things   the way they were.

C   G7   C
Now she's here, shining in the starlight.

         G7   C
Now she's here, suddenly I know.

F   Em
If she's here, it's crystal clear

   Am   D7   G7sus4 G7
I'm where I'm meant to go.

CHORUS 2

      F   C   G7   C
And at last I see the light, and it's like the fog has lifted.

      F   C   E7   Am
And at last I see the light, and it's like the sky is new.

       F   C   Em   G   F
And it's warm and real and bright, and the world has somehow shift - ed.

C   G7   C   F   G7 C C/B Am D7
All at once, ev'rything is different, now that I see you,

G7sus4 G7
now that I see

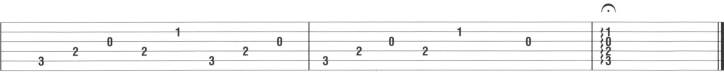

you.

Kiss the Girl

from THE LITTLE MERMAID
Music by Alan Menken
Lyrics by Howard Ashman

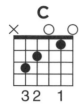 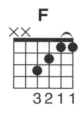  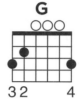

INTRO

Moderately

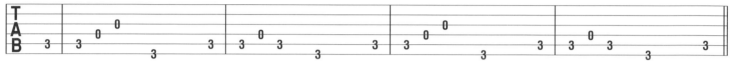

VERSE 1

C
　There you see her sitting there across the way.

F   C
She don't got a lot to say, but there's something about her.

　　　　　G7   C
And you don't know why, but you're dying to try. You wanna　kiss the girl.

VERSE 2

C
　Yes, you want her. Look at her, you know you do.

F   C
Possible she wants you, too. There is one way to ask her.

　　　　　G7   C
It don't take a word, not a single word, go on and　kiss the girl.

CHORUS 1

C   F   C   G7
Sha, la, la, la, la, la, my oh my. Look like the boy too shy. Ain't gonna　kiss the girl.

C   F   G   C
Sha, la, la, la, la, la, ain't that sad. Ain't it a shame, too bad. He gonna　miss the girl.

VERSE 3

C
Now's your moment, floating in a blue lagoon.

F   C
Boy, you better do it soon, no time will be better.

              G7   C
She don't say a word and she won't say a word until you   kiss the girl.

CHORUS 2

C   F   C   G7
  Sha, la, la, la, la, la, don't be scared. You got the mood prepared, go on and   kiss the girl.

C   F   G7   C
  Sha, la, la, la, la, la, don't stop now. Don't try to hide it how you wanna   kiss the girl.

                        F   C   G7
  Sha, la, la, la, la, la, float along. And listen to the song, the song say   kiss the girl.

C   F   G7   C
  Sha, la, la, la, la, the music play. Do what the music say. You gotta   kiss the girl.

OUTRO

              C
You've got to   kiss the girl.   You wanna   kiss the girl.

You've gotta   kiss the girl.   Go on and   kiss the girl.

Lava

from LAVA
Music and Lyrics by James Ford Murphy

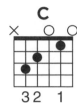 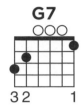 

INTRO

Fast

| C | | | G7 | | |
| F | | C | G7 | | ‖

VERSE 1

C   G7
A long, long time ago   there was a volcano

F   C   G7
living all alone in the middle of the sea.

C   G7
He sat high above his bay, watching all the couples play,

F   C   G7
and wishing that he had someone too.

C   G7
And from his lava came this song of hope that he sang

    F   C   G7
out loud ev'ry day for years and years.

CHORUS 1

F   C
"I have a dream I hope will come true,

   G7   C
that you're here with me, and I'm here with you.

  F   C
I wish that the earth, sea, and the sky up above-a

  F   G7   C
will send me someone to lava."

INTERLUDE 1

Slower

| F | | G7 | | C | | ‖

VERSE 2

C   G7
Years of singing all alone turned his lava into stone,

   F   C   G7
until he was on the brink of extinction.

C   G7
But little did he know that, living in the sea below,

   F   C   G7
another volcano was listening to his song.

C   G7
Ev'ry day she heard his tune, her lava grew and grew,

   F   C   G7
because she believed his song was meant for her.

C   G7
Now she was so ready to meet him above the sea,

   F   C   G7
as he sang his song of hope for the last time.

REPEAT CHORUS 1

INTERLUDE 2

| C | ‖

VERSE 3

C   G7
Rising from the sea below stood a lovely volcano,

F   C   G7
looking all around, but she could not see him.

   C   G7
He tried to sing to let her know that she was not there alone,

   F   C   G7
but with no lava his song was all gone.

   C   G7
He filled the sea with his tears, and watched his dreams disappear

   F   C   G7
as she remembered what his song meant to her.

REPEAT CHORUS 1

INTERLUDE 3

a tempo

| C | | | ‖

VERSE 4

C   G7
Oh, they were so happy to finally meet above the sea.

F   C   G7
All together now their lava grew and grew.

   C   G7
No longer are they all alone with aloha as their new home,

F   C   G7
and when you visit them this is what they sing.

OUTRO-CHORUS

F   C
"I have a dream I hope will come true,

   G7   C
that you'll grow old with me, and I'll grow old with you.

F   C
We thank the earth, sea, and the sky we thank too,

F G7   C
"I lava you."

F G7   C
"I lava you."

F G7   C
rit.
"I lava you."

Let It Go

from FROZEN
Music and Lyrics by Kristen Anderson-Lopez and Robert Lopez

(Capo 1st Fret)

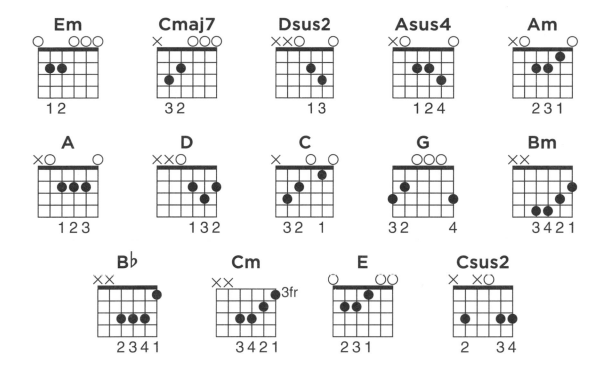

INTRO

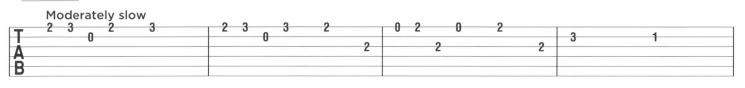

VERSE 1

Em   Cmaj7   Dsus2   Asus4 Am
The snow glows white on the mountain tonight; not a footprint to be seen.

Em   Cmaj7   Dsus2   Asus4 A
A kingdom of isolation, and it looks like I'm the queen.

Em   Cmaj7   Dsus2   Asus4 Am
The wind is howling like this swirling storm inside.

Em   Dsus2   Asus4 A
Couldn't keep it in, heaven knows I tried.

PRE-CHORUS 1

```
    D                               C
    Don't let them in, don't let them see;   be the good girl you always have to be.
    D                                 C                              N.C.
    Conceal, don't feel, don't let them know... Well, now they know.
```

CHORUS 1

```
          G        D      Em             C
    Let it go, let it go, can't hold it back anymore.
          G        D      Em             C
    Let it go, let it go, turn away and slam the door.
    G      D           Em      C
    I don't care what they're going to say.
          Bm        Bb     C                                G    D
    Let the storm rage on,   the cold never bothered me anyway.
```

VERSE 2

```
    Em                    C           D             Am
        It's funny how some distance makes everything seem small,
          Em              D          Asus4      A
    and the fears that once controlled me can't get to me at all.
```

PRE-CHORUS 2

```
    D                       C
        It's time to see what I can do, to test the limits and break through.
    D                             C          N.C.
    No right, no wrong, no rules for me,  I'm free!
```

CHORUS 2

```
          G        D    Em               C
    Let it go, let it go, I am one with the wind and sky.
          G        D    Em           C
    Let it go, let it go, you'll never see me cry.
    G    D        Em    C
    Here I stand, and here I'll stay,.
          Bm        Bb
    Let the storm rage on.
```

INTERLUDE

```
| C          |          |          |          ||
```

BRIDGE

C
My power flurries through the air into the ground.

My soul is spiraling in frozen fractals all around.

D
And one thought crystallizes like an icy blast;

E   C   D   Am   C   N.C.
I'm never going back. The past is in the past!

CHORUS 3

        G   D   Em   C
Let it go, let it go, and I'll rise like the break of dawn.

        G   D   Em   C
Let it go, let it go, that perfect girl is gone.

G   D   Em   C   Cm
Here I stand in the light of day,

       Bm   Bb   Csus2
Let the storm rage on,   the cold never bothered me anyway.

Remember Me
(Ernesto de la Cruz)

from COCO
Words and Music by Kristen Anderson-Lopez and Robert Lopez

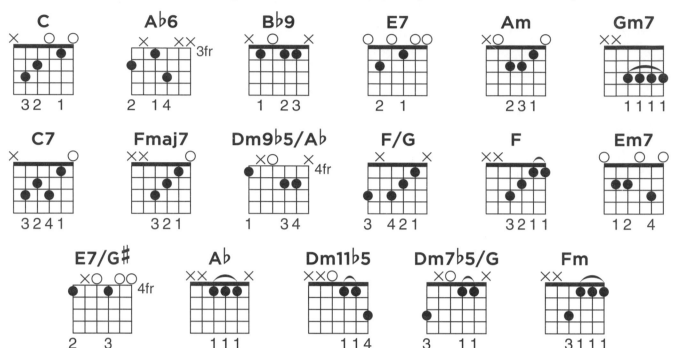

VERSE 1

Moderately

      C   Ab6
Remember me, though I have to say goodbye.

      C   Bb9   E7
Remember me, don't let it make you cry.

  Am   Gm7   C7
For even if I'm far away, I hold you in my heart.

Fmaj7   Dm9b5/Ab   F/G
I sing a secret song to you each night we are apart.

VERSE 2

      C   Ab6
Remember me, though I have to travel far.

      C   Gm7   C7
Remember me, each time you hear a sad guitar.

F   Em7   E7/G# Am Ab
Know that I'm with you the only way that I can   be.

Dm11b5   Dm7b5/G Ab   Fm C
Until you're in my arms again, re - mem - ber me.

You'll Be in My Heart (Pop Version)*

from TARZAN®
Words and Music by Phil Collins

(Capo 1st Fret)

F 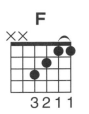   Bb 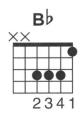   Gm 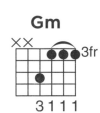   C 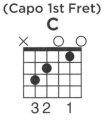   A    D 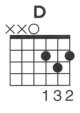   G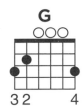

F#m7 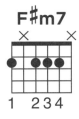   Bm    A7sus4 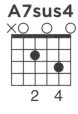   Gsus4 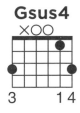   Gadd9 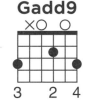   Emb6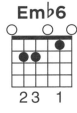

Em    Esus4    E 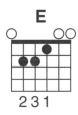   B 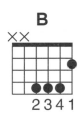   G#m7 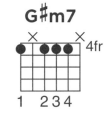   C#m

INTRO

Moderately

| **F** | | | | |

VERSE 1

F
Come stop your crying, it will be all right.

Just take my hand, hold it tight.

Bb
I will protect you from all around you.

Gm   **C**
I will be here, don't you cry.

VERSE 2

F
For one so small you seem so strong.

My arms will hold you, keep you safe and warm.

Bb
This bond between us can't be broken.

Gm   **C** **A**
I will be here, don't you cry.

CHORUS 1

```
          D              G          A          F#m7
'Cause you'll be in my heart, yes, you'll be in my heart

      Bm          G              C      A
from this day on, now and forevermore.
  D           G        A           F#m7
You'll be in my heart, no matter what they say.
         Bm         G        C       A7sus4  G   A
You'll be here in my heart always.
```

VERSE 3

```
  F
   Why can't they understand the way we feel?


They just don't trust what they can't explain.
  Bb
   I know we're different, but deep inside us

  Gm                       C     A
      we're not that different at all.
```

CHORUS 2

```
          D           G          A            F#m7
And you'll be in my heart, yes, you'll be in my heart

      Bm          G              C      A
from this day on, now and forevermore.
```

BRIDGE

```
      Gsus4  G         Gadd9      G
Don't listen to them, 'cause what do they know?
      Emb6      Em      Esus4   Em
We need each other to have, to hold.
    Bm            C
They'll see in time,  I  know.
      Gsus4  G         Gadd9  G
When destiny calls you, you must be strong.
  Emb6      Em              Esus4       Em
I may not be with you, but you've got to hold on.
    Bm            C
They'll see in time,  I  know.
        D        A
We'll show them together,
```

CHORUS 3

```
         E            A              B              G#m7
'cause    you'll be in my heart. Believe me, you'll be in my heart.

                   C#m         A            D    B
I'll be there from this day on, now and forevermore.

         E            A                          B              G#m7
Oo, you'll be in my heart, (You'll be here in my heart.) no matter what they say, (I'll be with you.)

         C#m          A                D    B
You'll be here in my heart (I'll be there.) always,

     A         E
always. I'll be with you.

         A                              E
I'll be there for you always, always and al - ways.

              A
Just look o - ver your shoulder.

              E
Just look o - ver your shoulder.

              A
Just look o - ver your shoulder.

              E
I'll be there always.
```

True Love's Kiss

from ENCHANTED
Music by Alan Menken
Lyrics by Stephen Schwartz

(Capo 3rd Fret)

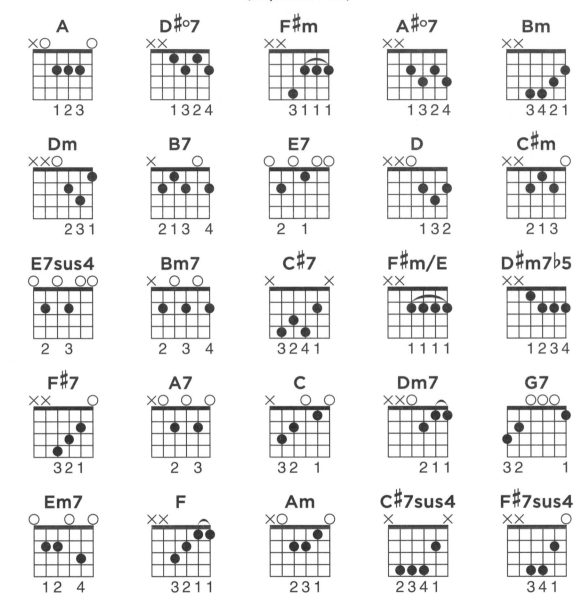

INTRO

Freely

        A   D#°7   A
Giselle: When you meet the someone who was meant for you,

   F#m   A#°7   Bm
before two can become one, there's something you must do.

             Dm   A   B7   E7
Bunny: Do you pull each other's tails? Bird: Do you feed each other seeds?

             D   A   F#m B7   E7
Giselle: No, there is something sweeter ev'ry - body needs.

VERSE 1

Moderately

```
A        C#m          D          A
I've been dreaming of a true love's kiss

D    E7  F#m              B7           E7
and a    prince I'm hoping comes with this.

D          A          F#m  B7      E7sus4  C#m  Bm7  E7
That's what brings everafter - ings so hap   -   py.

         A        C#m          D    A
And that's the reason we need lips so much,

D   E7  F#m          Bm          C#7
for lips  are the only things that touch.

F#m   F#m/E  D#m7b5  Dm       A
So, to spend a life of      endless bliss,

F#7                Bm7              E7sus4  E7
    just find who you love through true      love's
```

| A | C#m | D | A | D | E7 | F#m | A7 | ‖ |

kiss.

INTERLUDE

Fast, in 3

| D | | C#m | | Bm7 | | E7 | | |

| A | | D#°7 | | Bm7 | | E7 | | |
Ah,   ah,   ah.

| C | | D#°7 | | Dm7 | | G7 | | ‖ |
Ah,   ah,   ah.

VERSE 2

```
C        Em7          F          C
She's been dreaming of a true love's kiss

F    G7  Am              D           G7
and a    prince she's hoping comes with this.

F          Em7       Am  D   F   Em7  Dm7  E7
That's what brings everafter - ings so hap - py, so hap  -  py.

         A        C#m          D    A
And that's the reason we need lips so much,

D   E7  F#m          B7          C#7sus4  C#7
for lips  are the only things that touch.
```

OUTRO

A tempo, in 4

```
F#m   F#m/E  D#m7b5  Dm       A
So, to spend a life of      endless bliss,

F#7sus4    F#7     Bm7              E7sus4  E7   A
    just find who you love through true      love's kiss.
```

When She Loved Me

from TOY STORY 2
Music and Lyrics by Randy Newman

(Capo 5th Fret)

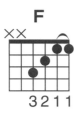

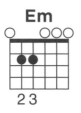
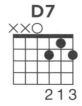
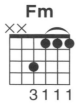
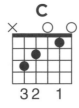

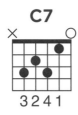

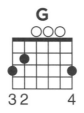
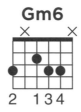
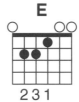

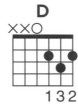
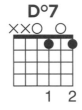
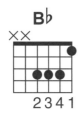
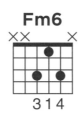
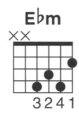
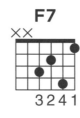

INTRO

Moderately slow

| Am   Em | D7   Fm | C | | ‖

VERSE 1

```
C         Dm7 C     F     D7      Gsus4   G
```
When somebody loved me, ev'ry - thing was beautiful

```
Bm7♭5  E       Am        C F           G
```
Ev'ry   hour we spent together lives within my heart.

VERSE 2

```
C         Dm7 C F   D7      Gsus4 G
```
And when she was sad, I was there to dry her tears.

```
Bm7♭5  E       Am  C   F   C G7  C
```
And when she was happy, so was I when she loved me.

BRIDGE 1

```
F                                    C        Gm7  C7      F
Through the summer and the fall, we had each other, that was all.

     C      F   C     D7                   G7
Just she and I together,     like it was meant to be.
```

VERSE 3

```
C         Dm7   C    F    D7      Gsus4    G
And when she was lonely, I was there to comfort her,

     C7    F    C   G7    C
And I knew that she loved me.
```

BRIDGE 2

```
Am             Gm6         C      D    D°7   C    Cm
So the years went by, I stayed the same. But she began to drift away,

B♭    E    Am  Fm6 G     E♭m    F7
I was left alone. Still I waited for the day

            D♭6         E♭m   G7
when she'd say, "I will always love   you."
```

VERSE 4

```
C    Dm7   C    F    D7           Gsus4    G
Lonely and forgotten, never thought she'd look my way,

     Bm7♭5   E      Am    C    F            G
And she smiled at me and held me   just like she used to do,

     C7    F           C    G7
like she loved me when she loved me.
```

OUTRO

```
C         Dm7  C     F    D7      Gsus4    G
When somebody loved me, ev'ry - thing was beautiful

Bm7♭5  E      Am         C  F          G         C  G7   C
Ev'ry     hour we spent together lives within my heart when she loved me.
```

A Whole New World

from ALADDIN
Music by Alan Menken
Lyrics by Tim Rice

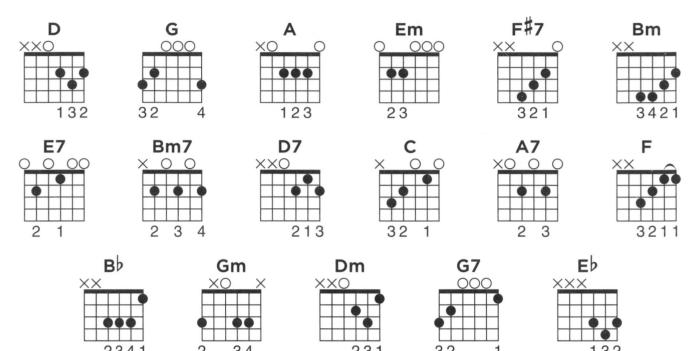

VERSE 1

Moderately

       D   G   A

Aladdin: I can show you the world, shining shimmering, splen - did.

Em   F#7   Bm   G   D

Tell me princess, now when did you last let your heart decide?

VERSE 2

D   G   A

I can open your eyes, take you wonder by won - der,

Em   F#7   Bm   G   D

over, sideways and under on a magic carpet ride.

CHORUS 1

                  A   D   A   D

A whole new world,   a new fantastic point of view.

                  G   D   G   D   Bm7   E7   G

No one to tell us no or where to go or say we're only dreaming.

                       A   D   A   F#7   Bm

Jasmine: A whole new world,   a dazzling place I never knew.

D7   G   D   G   D   Bm7   E7 C   A7

But, when I'm way up here, it's crystal clear that now I'm in a whole new world with

           D

           you.

Aladdin: Now I'm in a whole new world with

VERSE 3

         F   Bb   C

Jasmine: Unbelievable sights, indescribable feel - ing.
          you.

Gm   A7   Dm   Bb   F

Soaring, tumbling, freewheeling through an endless diamond sky.

CHORUS 2

              C   F   C   F

A whole new world,   a hundred thousand things to see.

          Bb   F   Bb   F   Dm   G7   Bb   C

I'm like a shooting star, I've come so far, I can't go back to where I used to be.

BRIDGE

               F   C   A7   Dm   F   Bb   F

Every turn a surprise.   Every moment red letter. I'll chase them any - where.

        Bb   F   Dm   G7   Eb   C   Dm   F

There's time to spare. Let me share this whole new world with you.

OUTRO

               Bb   F   Gm   F

           Jasmine: A whole new world,   that's where we'll be.
Aladdin: A whole new world,   that's where we'll be.

       Bb   C   F

         A wonderous place for you and me.
A thrilling chase   for you and me.

Yo Ho
(A Pirate's Life for Me)

from DISNEY PARKS' PIRATES OF THE CARIBBEAN ATTRACTION
Words by Xavier Atencio
Music by George Bruns

(Capo 5th Fret)

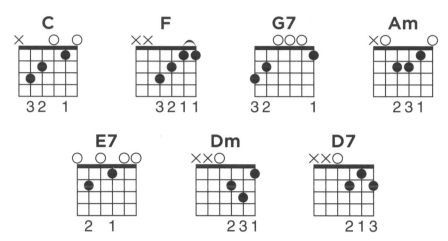

VERSE 1

Moderately

```
C      F  C          G7   C
```
Yo ho, yo ho, a pirate's life for me.

```
   Am                    E7
```
We pillage, we plunder, we rifle and loot.

```
   Am                    E7
```
Drink up me 'earties, yo ho.

```
   Dm        G7        C           Am
```
We kidnap and ravage and don't give a hoot.

```
    D7              G7
```
Drink up me 'earties, yo ho.

VERSE 2

```
C      F  C          G7   C
```
Yo ho, yo ho, a pirate's life for me.

```
   Am                    E7
```
We extort and pilfer, we filch and sack.

```
   Am                    E7
```
Drink up me 'earties, yo ho.

```
   Dm        G7        C     Am
```
Maraud and embezzle and even hijack.

```
    D7              G7
```
Drink up me 'earties, yo ho.

VERSE 3

```
C      F  C          G7    C
Yo ho, yo ho, a pirate's life for me.

      Am                 E7
We kindle and char and inflame and ignite.

      Am                 E7
Drink up me 'earties, yo ho.

      Dm          G7        C      Am
We burn up the city, we're really a fright.

      D7             G7
Drink up me 'earties, yo ho.
```

VERSE 4

```
      Am                 E7
We're rascals, scoundrels, villains and knaves.

      Am                 E7
Drink up me 'earties, yo ho.

      Dm         G7        C      Am
We're devils and black sheep, really bad eggs.

      D7             G7
Drink up me 'earties, yo ho.
```

VERSE 5

```
C      F  C          G7    C
Yo ho, yo ho, a pirate's life for me.

      Am                      E7
We're beggars and blighters and ne'er-do-well cads.

      Am                 E7
Drink up me 'earties, yo ho.

Dm           G7        C        Am
Aye, but we're loved by our mommies and dads.

      D7             G7
Drink up me 'earties, yo ho.
```

OUTRO

```
C      F  C          G7    C
Yo ho, yo ho, a pirate's life for me.
```

You've Got a Friend in Me

from TOY STORY
Music and Lyrics by Randy Newman

(Capo 1st Fret)

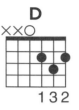 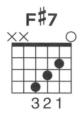 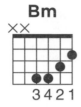 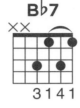 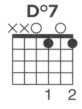 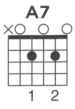

D   F#7   Bm   Bb7   D°7   A7

 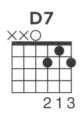 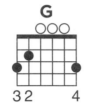 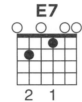 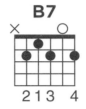 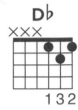

A7#5   D7   G   E7   B7   Db

 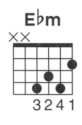 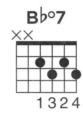  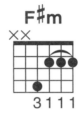

D6   Ebm   Bb°7   F#m   Em

INTRO

Moderately

| D   F#7 | Bm   Bb7 | D   D°7 A7 | D | | ‖

VERSE 1

D   A7#5   D7
You've got a friend in me.

G   D°7   D
You've got a friend in me.

G   D   F#7   Bm
When the road looks   rough ahead

     G   D   F#7   Bm
and you're miles and miles from your nice warm bed,

G   D   F#7   Bm
   you just remember what your old pal said,

   E7   A7   D   B7
"Boy, you've got a friend in me.

   E7   A7
Yeah, you've got a friend in me."

INTERLUDE

| D   F#7 | Bm   Bb7 | D   D°7 A7 | ‖

VERSE 2

D   A7♯5   D7
  You've got a friend in me.

G   D°7   D
  You've got a friend in me.

G   D   F♯7   Bm
  You got troubles, then I got 'em too.

G   D   F♯7   Bm
  There isn't anything I wouldn't do for you.

G   D   F♯7   Bm
If we stick together we can see it through,

     E7   A7   D B7
'cause, you've got a friend in me.

E7   A7   D
  You've got a friend in me.

BRIDGE

G   D♭
  Now, some other folks might be a little smarter that I am,

D6   D°7   D6
  Bigger and stronger, too.   Maybe.

D♭   E♭m   B♭°7 D♭   F♯m B7
  But none of them will ever love you the way I do,

   Em   A7
just me and you, boy.

VERSE 3

D   A7♯5   D7
  And as the years go by,

  G   D°7   D
our friendship will never die.

G   D°7   D   Bm
  You're gonna see it's our destin - y.

E7   A7   D B7
  You've got a friend in me.

E7   A7   D B7
  You've got a friend in me.

E7   A7
  You've got a friend in me.

OUTRO

| D   F♯7 | Bm   B♭7 | D   D°7 A7 | D |